# The
# Donald Orrs:
## Missionary Duet

### LEE HOLLAWAY
#### Illustrated by Dick Wahl

**BROADMAN PRESS**
**Nashville, Tennessee**

**To**

**Ernest Lee and Ida Nelle Hollaway,**

**whose hearts have always been**

**on the mission field**

© Copyright 1983 • Broadman Press

All rights reserved.

4242-83

ISBN: 0-8054-4283-9

Dewey Decimal Classification: J266.092

Subject Headings: ORR, DONALD / / ORR, VIOLET / /

MISSIONS—COLOMBIA / / MISSIONS, MUSIC

Library of Congress Catalog Card Number: 82-73666

Printed in the United States of America

# Contents

# From Backstage to Boom Town

"The show will just have to go on without us tonight!"

"But Buck," his brother complained, "you know you are the best comedian in the troupe!"

"It doesn't matter," Buck replied firmly. "Hazel is having her baby tonight—probably any minute now. Somebody else in the family can fill in with an extra song or a juggling act."

"OK, OK! We'll come up with something. Anyway, I hope everything goes all right for Hazel."

"Thanks! Say, what is the name of this town?"

"I think they call it Verden."

"What a way to come into the world," said Buck, shaking his head. "My first child is going to be born in an upstairs room in the only hotel in Verden, Oklahoma. And all the relatives will be singing and dancing right through the whole thing!"

Buck was one of eight children in the Rogers family. They and their father and mother were traveling entertainers. They were constantly moving from one little town to another. After one or two shows in one place, they would move on down the road. Each member of the family had a part in the show—singing, playing an instrument, painting scenery, or something—to help make their audiences happy.

When little Violet Rogers was born later that evening, her first

**5**

bed was a pillow laid inside a dresser drawer. In fact, that was the only kind of bed she had until she grew too big to fit in a drawer. Then she slept on a pallet or shared the big bed with her parents.

By the time Violet—called "Vi" for short—was three years old, Grandpa Rogers thought she should start doing her part in the show.

"Sometimes we need to change clothes between acts or move things around on the stage," he told her. "You can give us a little extra time by standing in front of the curtain and singing the folks a little song."

"But what should I sing, Grandpa?" Vi asked.

"It doesn't really matter," he told her. "Whatever you sing, Child, they will love it!"

A few nights later a little girl with dark hair and a pretty pink dress was gently shoved onto the stage. Only the people in the first two rows could hear her sing "My Bonnie Lies Over the Ocean." But the people clapped anyway, and Vi bowed. Each time after that she sang a little louder.

Not many months later Buck decided it was time to take his family out of the troupe and settle down. Besides Vi, there was also Baby Gene. So Buck moved to the small town of Helena, Oklahoma, and went into business cleaning and pressing people's clothes.

Their house on the edge of town was small, but it was special to Vi because it was her first real home. There was plenty of room for her and Gene to run and play outside. She liked the smooth, soft feel of the dust beneath her feet. And if she wanted to see her dad during the day, she could go to his shop which was less than a block away.

Buck had never had much time or interest for God or the church. Sometime during their second year in Helena, however, Hazel talked him into attending a revival meeting at one of the churches. As he listened to the preacher that night, Buck began to

**6**

realize how badly he needed God in his life. Before the night was over, Buck surrendered his life to God.

God's presence became extremely important to the Rogers family just a short while later. When Vi was five years old, her mother died suddenly. The young family carried Hazel's body by train to her family home in Indiana. On their way back to Oklahoma, they rode in the rumble seat of Vi's aunt and uncle's car. Buck was staring up at the stars and praying, wondering what he would do with his life. Suddenly he felt God telling him, "I want your life to serve me!"

Buck answered God's call quickly and enthusiastically. He believed that serving God meant getting the right kind of training and education. An eighth-grade education had seemed like enough before, but now he felt that he needed high school and college. Soon after their return to Helena, he moved the Rogers family to Shawnee, home of Oklahoma Baptist University, so he could begin his studies.

Almost immediately Buck began preaching in "half-time churches," churches which held services only twice a month. Vi and Gene usually went with him.

One Sunday Buck preached a strong sermon about hell, telling how terrible it was. At the close of the service, Vi went forward to say she surely did not want to go there!

On another Sunday about three years later, when Vi was ten, she felt that her dad was preaching right to her. She realized for the first time that she needed to accept Jesus as her own Savior. It was tough to go forward since she knew no one in that church, but she knew she had to go.

That evening, on the way back to Shawnee, Vi told her dad, "I really know my life is going to be different from now on. You know how much I hate to do dishes. But after Sunday dinner at that lady's house today, I *volunteered* to help with the dishes. That just proves that Jesus is already changing my life!"

Being raised by one parent was not easy for Vi and Gene. No one had much money in those days. A father who was a student and a part-time preacher had less than most people. Buck knew how to fix fried potatoes and cream gravy, so they ate that a lot. They also ate lots of black-eyed peas. And Vi often took dried, hard biscuits to school for lunch. Their "good meals" were when they got the leftovers from the girls' dormitory at the college.

In addition to going to churches with her dad, Vi sometimes went to classes with him. In fact, one of the students at the college, a missionary's daughter from China, gave Vi her first piano lessons.

During Vi's tenth summer, when they had been in Shawnee about five years, Buck decided they should take a family vacation.

"Your Aunt Babe and Uncle Lad left the family troupe and moved to Texas about the time you were born," he told Vi. "Let's just load up the old jalopy and pay them a visit!"

The trip to Big Spring was long and hot. Gene was very fussy by the time they got to the home of Buck's sister. Getting to know these family members was fun, though, so Vi and her dad and brother settled in for a good, long visit.

"It's hard to get used to thinking of you as a preacher," Uncle Lad told Buck. "I keep remembering you singing and telling jokes on stage!"

"Do you suppose there is a little church around here that needs someone to preach for them?" Buck asked. "I might be able to help them out and give you a demonstration at the same time."

Sure enough, there was such a church. Soon that church asked him to preach for them on a regular basis. Then he found out about a full-time job in a cleaning and pressing shop in the nearby town of Midland. Their summer vacation was turning into a permanent move!

After their move to Midland, Buck and Vi and Gene started attending the First Baptist Church there. But Buck was not happy "sitting on the sidelines."

"Surely there is some place I could serve the Lord," Buck told the pastor.

"Let me suggest a place," said the pastor. "Our church has a little Spanish mission that meets on Sunday afternoons. We could use you to work in it and maybe even become the mission pastor."

"But I don't speak Spanish!" Buck protested.

"You can use an interpreter while you are learning," the pastor replied. "And I know just the person to teach you! Miss Annie Lee King can be your private tutor."

Miss King, a rancher's daughter from Midland, taught first grade in the public school. She had been leading a Bible class at the Spanish mission. She agreed to give Buck Spanish lessons in the evenings.

For a while it seemed to Vi that she was not getting to see her dad much. By the time she got home from school and he got home from work, they had time only for a quick supper before he had to go to his class. His spare time on weekends was spent working with the mission.

Then one evening Vi was surprised by an invitation.

"Why don't you come to my Spanish class with me? I've been wanting you kids to meet Miss King," said their dad.

In less than an hour, the three of them were climbing the porch steps of a frame house. It was already dark, but the lamp from the living room lit up the curly, red hair of the woman who met them at the door. To Vi that hair looked like a halo around her head. Vi had prayed for five years for a new mother, and she wondered, "Could this be the one?"

When they all got inside, Vi learned that beneath that red hair was a beautiful smile. Not much Spanish was learned that night, but they had a good time getting to know one another!

"Well, what did you think of her?" Buck asked when they were finally home again.

"She seemed very nice!" said Vi enthusiastically.

"Nice enough to become your new mother?"

"Oh, yes! She would be perfect!" Vi squealed in delight.

And so Miss King became Mrs. Rogers. Within a year, the four members of the Rogers family moved a little further west. Buck became pastor of a church right in the middle of an oil-drilling camp just outside of the booming town of Odessa.

Buck's preaching brought a response from Vi again when she was thirteen. After a stirring sermon about mission needs around the world, Vi committed her life to mission service.

As Vi told Buck of her decision at the close of the service, he seemed a little shaken.

"Are you sure, Honey?" he asked. "I really hadn't thought about *you* being the one to go!"

Vi was serious about her decision, and she never forgot it. But becoming a missionary meant to her becoming a preacher, teacher, doctor, or nurse. She never had thought much about medicine as a vocation. From among those choices, though, Vi thought she would prefer to go as a missionary doctor.

# Just One of the Gang

At about the same time that Violet Rogers was being born in a hotel in Oklahoma, Don Orr was singing in church for the first time in Arkansas.

Don was just four years old when he and his two-year-old sister Nancy sang their first "duet" in Central Baptist Church in Hot Springs. The church was meeting in a high school auditorium then, but it was already very important to the Orr family. Don's parents, Roy and Lola Mae, were some of the first members of that church. Both of them sang in the choir and taught in the Sunday School.

Perhaps that early experience put a "label" on Don. At least he was asked to sing many times after that as he grew through childhood and youth.

"God has given you a beautiful voice," his parents told him. "We hope you will always use it for him."

Getting to church often was difficult for the Orrs when Don was in the third through eighth grades. First, Don's father bought and then lost a paint and wallpaper store in a nearby town. Then the family moved to a farm, where they could raise much of their own food. Of course Don, as the oldest, got a good share of the chores. The arrival of a new sister, Mary Ann, and brother, Bob, added to family responsibilities too.

The family moved back to town about the time Don entered high

**11**

school. Then he was able to take on some paying jobs. His first job was chipping cement off bricks so they could be used again. Later he used his bicycle to cover a 21-mile afternoon paper route.

Music and church activities continued to be at the center of Don's life. He sang in the glee club in both junior high and high school. When he was still in the ninth grade (which was part of the junior high in Hot Springs), Don was invited to sing in the high school quartet. He sang first tenor with that group for four years. At church it just seemed natural for Don to be the music director during Youth Week.

The young people Don was with at church usually were the ones he was with at other times during the week. This group enjoyed being together and doing things together, so they kept something going all the time.

"What shall we do this week?" someone would ask after church on Sunday night.

"How about a hayride?" came one suggestion. "We haven't done that in a while."

"It's still too hot! Let's save that for the fall!"

"Then how about the lake?"

"Lake Catherine or Lake Hamilton?"

"I like Hamilton best. Let's meet at the marina at ten o'clock Saturday morning."

"That sounds great! And don't forget that our Training Union group has the roller-skating rink reserved for our party Thursday evening!"

And so it would go. Many times when there were no special activities planned, some of them would gather at someone's house for Ping-Pong, Monopoly, or Parcheesi.

Even Sundays involved more than just Sunday School and church. At the close of the morning service, Don often went looking for his mother, with two friends right behind him.

"Mom, can Arvis and Bub have Sunday dinner with us?" Don

**13**

would ask. On another Sunday it might be John or Matthew.

Mrs. Orr would almost always answer, "Yes, that will be fine, as long as their folks know where they are."

Sunday dinner generally was the biggest meal of the week. It included one or two kinds of meat, perhaps a half dozen vegetables, salad, bread, and at least a couple of different desserts. That was not the kind of meal one could rush through—or would want to!

Once all their food had settled, Don and his friends frequently climbed West Mountain, which was behind his house. It was not very big, as mountains go, but it was steep and rocky enough that it took about an hour to reach the top. Then they would climb down the other side to reach the home of another friend. It just happened that this friend's father managed a milk and ice cream factory! That made it the perfect place to stop for a cool snack after their climb. And when they finished there, they would all head back to church for Training Union and the evening worship service.

During Don's year in the tenth grade he heard a lot about Siloam Springs. People said it was a beautiful camp up in the middle of the Ozark Mountains. Even more important to Don, they said that special preachers, teachers, and musicians were part of a one-week program there each summer.

"Do you suppose I could go to Siloam Springs this summer, Dad?" Don asked, even though he knew the answer.

"We don't have any money for that sort of thing," his father replied. "Going is one thing—I would be happy for you to get to go—but paying for it is another. We just can't afford it!"

"Since I don't have money to pay for camp," Don thought, "I wonder if I could get a job there for that week."

Don found out there were several jobs available at the camp. As it turned out, he was able to get a job serving tables in the dining room. His pay just covered his expenses for the week. Don thought it was such a good deal that he did it again the following summer!

In addition to the outstanding program, Don enjoyed getting to meet people from many other places. Among these was a group of college students who had been assigned the job of "summer field-workers." Don and one of his favorite cousins, Arvis Brooks, became especially interested in this program.

"Just what does a summer field-worker do, anyway?" Arvis asked one of the students.

"Mostly we go around to small, rural churches and try to help them get Training Unions started," said the student.

"I ought to be pretty good at that," exclaimed Don. "It seems like I've been in Training Union all my life!"

"Actually you are supposed to have been to college at least one year," the student continued. "But you might have a chance at it next summer, when you finish high school. You see they like to send a team of a boy and a girl to each church. The fact is, though, they have trouble getting as many boys as they need."

"Well, let's give it a try!" said Arvis enthusiastically. "What do you say, Don?"

Don agreed.

During their senior year in high school, both boys submitted applications to the program for that summer. As the student had predicted, a shortage of boys persuaded the program directors to accept the two cousins a year early.

Each week of their fieldwork followed a similar pattern. A group of the workers would be taken into an area on Saturday afternoon. Then they would split up into teams to go to different churches. After Sunday morning services, they would bring a group from their churches to a rally that afternoon. The rest of the week would be spent teaching a study course and trying to organize a Training Union.

As the summer neared an end, Don and Arvis got together to compare notes.

"I guess you will be heading for Ouachita [WASH-i-taw] College in a few weeks," said Arvis.

Don nodded. "Yes, it's only thirty-five miles from home, but I know it will be a different experience for me. This summer has helped convince me that God wants me in his service somewhere. I know a Baptist college will help me prepare for that. But I sure wish I knew exactly what kind of work it will be. It's hard for me to imagine myself as a preacher!"

# Getting Ready for God's Work

Don started to Ouachita College in the fall of 1939. Like many families at that time, the Orrs still did not have much money. Don paid most of his school bills by working at various jobs on the campus.

During the week he worked as a "kitchen boy" in the cafeteria. He spent at least two hours at every mealtime helping prepare and serve the food.

On Saturdays he worked on the college farm. Sometimes he had to help kill and butcher hogs. Other times he had to peel potatoes.

One of the things Don enjoyed most during his first year in college was singing in the Ouachita choir. The choir often made trips by bus to sing at churches or for special meetings. During his second year, Don became the assistant bus driver. Then he became head bus driver the year after that.

Don had always had an interest in mechanical things, especially cars and trucks. For a summer job Don worked on a dump truck, hauling materials for construction work on the campus. One day the driver of the heavy truck got it stuck in the soft dirt near the river. He was so angry that he finally walked off and left the truck there. Don got behind the wheel and worked and worked with the truck until he managed to get it free. Soon after that he was asked to be the regular driver of the truck.

In addition to buses and trucks, Don was interested in airplanes. All through high school he had watched them landing

and taking off at the Hot Springs airport. As he was starting his third year in college, he learned about a way he could get flying lessons free!

"It's called Civilian Pilot Training—CPT for short," Don told his roommate. "The government will pay for all of your ground classes—you know, navigation, weather, basic maintenance, things like that. Then they will pay for your flying lessons too!"

"What's the catch?" his roommate wanted to know. "What does the government get out of the deal?"

"Well, you do have to agree to go into the Air Corps later, but that is only if you are needed," said Don. "And this program is all over the country. How many pilots could they possibly use?"

Don began the CPT program in September, 1941, and successfully earned his pilot's license.

On Sunday, December 7, he was on a choir trip to a nearby town when they heard an announcement on the radio: "The Japanese today attacked Pearl Harbor in the Hawaiian Islands!" Everyone was shocked. It was several days before Don realized how this would affect his life. The United States was soon at war. At the end of that school term, Don was called upon to enter the Air Corps.

"We will give you a choice," the Air Corps trainers told him. "We can teach you to be either a fighter pilot or a bomber pilot."

Most of the men chose bombers since those planes were larger and had two or more engines. Don had his own private reason for choosing fighters. He had discovered that his stomach got a little uneasy when someone else was piloting. When he was at the controls, however, he never had a problem. So he took his training on the P-47 "Thunderbolt," a single-engine, one-pilot plane.

One of his first assignments was to go to India to train British pilots in the flying of the P-47. Then after a brief time in China, he took part in the invasion of Burma. Altogether he flew 203 combat missions. This was the second highest number of missions among pilots in that area at that time.

**19**

Not all of Don's missions went smoothly. Many times other planes on the same mission were shot down or crashed. Once he had a tire to blow out during takeoff, but he was able to land the plane without flipping over and burning. Once he had a bomb stuck under one wing. Usually when a pilot tried to land like that the bomb would come loose and blow up the plane. In Don's case, however, the bomb had a delayed fuse, so he got away safely. He often wondered why he was spared. "Why did I live when some of my friends did not," he questioned. Somehow he wanted to use his life in a special way to serve God.

When the war was over, Don returned to Ouachita for his final year of college. He now felt that preparing to serve God meant that he should go on to seminary. He thought God's work for him might be as a minister of music or education in a church. Don had been singing in public since the age of four. But he took his first formal music course—a course in music history—during his last year at Ouachita.

Violet Rogers enrolled at East Texas Baptist College (ETBC) with the idea of studying medicine. That was what she needed to do in order to become a missionary doctor. Her first two science courses convinced her, however, that her talent was in other areas. Her part-time job as a nurse's aide was interesting, but that was not the way she wanted to spend the rest of her life.

Vi continued to enjoy her music, so she turned in that direction in her studies. She spent a lot of time practicing her singing. She sang solos every chance she got, especially in religious services. When she finished the two-year program at ETBC, she went on to Baylor University, in Waco, Texas. In addition to studying music, she took some courses in teaching. Vi spent lots of time going out with student revival teams. She also sang in a trio with Bennie May Oliver, a missionary's daughter from Brazil, and her best friend, Eva Marie Kennard. During her last year at Baylor, Vi served as choir director for one of the local churches.

While Vi was attending college, her dad moved to California to do pioneer missions work. His experience in entertainment had helped Buck develop an ability to meet new people. He used that ability in helping get a new church started.

Vi joined her family after graduation. She took a job teaching in a junior high school in the Los Angeles area. In her spare time, she studied voice in Hollywood and thought about a career in opera or musical comedy. She also sang on a Sunday morning radio program and worked with youth and music in her dad's church.

An announcement by the San Francisco Opera Company excited some of Vi's friends. The company was auditioning singers to go on tour with them.

"You ought to try it!" Vi's friends insisted. "Your soprano voice is strong enough to make it in opera!"

Vi had plenty of doubts about that. But to quiet her friends—and satisfy her own curiosity—she agreed to audition. On the day announced, she sang for the judges. Later that day Vi learned that she was among those chosen. Suddenly she found she was going to have to make an important decision within a few days.

Vi's whole family shared in her concern. Memories of his own years on the road came to Buck's mind as he thought of Vi joining the opera company. Still he knew that the choice had to be hers alone.

Vi had dreamed of singing opera, but her church work was important to her too. Finally she decided, "God has first claim on my life. I'm going to stay right here—at least for this year!"

The following summer, Eva Marie, Vi's roommate from Baylor, came to California. The two of them did some missions work together. In the evenings they talked about what they were going to do with their lives.

"In a way, I guess I envy you," Vi told her friend. "I mean, you know that you want to do student work, and that's that."

"And right here in California wouldn't be a bad place for it either!"

"I wish I could be that sure!"

"What do you *want* to do?" asked Eva Marie.

"It's got to be in music—I'm sure of that! And yet I still get goose pimples when I hear missionary stories. How can those two things go together? And then there's all the work to be done in churches right around here. I just don't know!"

"I'll pray with you that you will have an answer before this summer is over," Eva Marie promised.

A book helped bring Vi closer to an answer. Someone lent her a copy of *The Splendor of God*, a biography of Ann and Adoniram Judson, two of the first American foreign missionaries. One night it was so hot Vi could not sleep. She sat on the screened-in porch all night and read about the Judsons. She was deeply touched by their example of dedicated service. Through reading the book, Vi felt again God's call to mission service. But she thought, "How can a musician get to the mission field?"

As the summer neared an end, Vi continued to struggle with what direction her life should go now. She prayed hard that God would show her his will. Eva Marie and Buck and others prayed with her.

"Well, what's it going to be?" Buck asked her at last.

Vi smiled. "I guess I can't escape being my dad's daughter," she said. "God has given me your talent for music—and I suppose I will always have a little of the stage ham in me too. Yet the greatest joy I have known has been to see God move through the use of my voice to touch people's hearts for him. Somehow, somewhere, I believe he wants me to use this talent in his service. That's why I'll be going to Fort Worth, Texas, this fall to enroll in Southwestern Seminary!"

# A Call to Colombia

"TRYOUTS FOR SOUTHWESTERN SINGERS, 2:00 PM TODAY," read the notice on the bulletin board.

Vi hurried to the music hall a little early so she could get a seat near the front. Certainly she was going to try out for this traveling student choir. She also wanted to hear every one of the other applicants sing.

Only a certain number could be chosen. It soon looked as though twice that many had come for the tryouts. Vi recognized quite a number of fellow students from the school of music. At least some, she supposed, were enrolled in the schools of theology or religious education. Hearing all these special people sing promised to be a real treat!

Each person had to sing a brief solo. Many of the voices were truly beautiful. Vi enjoyed listening, especially to the women singers, and couldn't help wondering if she would be chosen. The others were so good!

One of the male singers caught her attention too. He was a tall, young man with a lovely tenor voice. The pants he wore obviously had been part of a military uniform. His name was Donald Orr.

At the conclusion of the auditions, one of the teaching assistants announced: "A list of those selected will be posted by the dean's door tomorrow. I need to see the following people before you leave today."

**25**

He read eight names, and both Vi's and Don's were among them.

When everyone else had left, the teaching assistant explained: "I have no doubt that each of you will be chosen for the Singers. Right now, though, we need your help with something else. We have a radio program on one of the local stations every Sunday morning. We want the eight of you to sing as a double quartet. It won't be anything very fancy—mostly just hymns you have been singing all your life. Oh, and it will be early enough so you can make it on to your churches. Any problems?"

No one raised a hand.

"Fine. Then we will see you there at 7:30 next Sunday morning—air time is at 8:00. Check with me if you need directions to the studio."

Vi rode to the studio with one of the other girls from her dormitory. Getting back to the campus might be a bit of a problem, though, since the girl was going straight to her church on the other side of town.

The radio program went off without a hitch. Vi thought they sounded very good for a group that had not had even one rehearsal!

"Anyone need a ride out to Seminary Hill?" Don asked as they headed for the door.

"I do, thanks," said Vi, relieved to have her transportation problem solved so easily.

"Anyone else?"

"I've got a church choir to direct," said one.

"I just have time to get to my Sunday School class," said another.

"It looks like you and I must be the only first-year students in the group," Don told Vi as he headed his 1939 Buick toward the school. "Everyone else already has some church responsibility."

"I don't expect it will take long for us to find our place too," said Vi. "But right now I am still trying to decide on a church to join. Today I thought I would visit Travis Avenue Baptist Church."

Don dropped Vi off at the women's dorm and went to his room to get dressed for church. About a half hour later he started out in his car again, still not sure where he would go for worship.

As he pulled up to a stop sign, he saw Vi standing at a bus stop.

"Are you still going to Travis Avenue?" he called.

She nodded.

"Then hop in," he said. "I think I will visit there today too."

Sunday School was almost half over when they reached the church. Rather than disturb a class, Vi and Don sat in the church's large auditorium and read together the verses being used in the lesson for that day.

Since both Don and Vi were voice students at the seminary, they saw each other almost daily after that. It was almost a month, however, before they had their first date. Then they began doing things together regularly. Several times they were invited to sing duets in nearby churches. By April they had become engaged, and in July of 1948 they were married.

Somehow Vi never got around to talking to Don about her earlier missions call. Don was definitely preparing for service as a minister of music. In fact, he was already serving as minister of music at Westside Baptist Church. As his wife, she expected to continue to be involved in the music program of a local church somewhere.

Students at Southwestern Seminary could not very well forget about missions however. Twice each year there was a special chapel service called Missionary Day in which a "real, live missionary" usually spoke.

On one particular Missionary Day both Don and Vi arrived late, coming from separate classes. The auditorium was so full that they had to find separate seats in the balcony.

Missionary Harry Schweinsberg was the speaker. He told about needs in Colombia, a country in South America. As the missionary spoke, Don felt himself getting angry. Looking around at the

**29**

hundreds of preachers in the audience, he thought, "Can't they see the need in other countries? Why do they want to just stay in America? Isn't the Lord speaking to them?"

Then the missionary said something that stopped Don short. "We have a special need in Colombia for a missionary with training in music. Our young churches need to know how to use music in worship, as a way to share their faith."

Don felt God say to him, "That's *you* the missionary is talking about. I want *you* to go!"

"This just can't be," Don thought. "Who ever heard of a music missionary? And besides, Vi and I have never talked about going to another country to serve God."

On the other side of the balcony, Vi also had listened carefully to the missionary. She heard him tell about the thousands of people waiting anxiously for someone to share the good news of Jesus with them. She thought, "How wonderful it would be to be the first person ever to tell people about Jesus! But I can't do that! I'm married now, and Don has never said anything about missionary service."

After Mr. Schweinsberg finished, Dr. Edwin McNeely, Don and Vi's voice teacher, came to the platform. He told the students, "I cannot go to Colombia. But I have prepared some of you to go!"

Vi felt he was talking right to her. As the invitation hymn continued, she thought, "God, I hope you know what you are doing because I surely don't understand. I just know that I have to answer your call!"

As she stepped into the aisle, she bumped into someone. It was Don! He also had felt and surrendered to God's call. They joined hands and went forward together to pledge themselves to missionary service.

Don was very sure of his call from God to be a music missionary. This was a new idea for most people, though, including the Foreign Mission Board. They said they would be glad for him to go as a

**30**

missionary if he prepared himself to go as a preacher. Don told them he was not called as a preacher but to work in music.

This discussion continued by mail and telephone for two and one-half years. Finally Don neared the end of his seminary studies. Again he contacted the Foreign Mission Board. This time, however, he received some encouragement. Policies were changing, they told him. Besides, the missionaries in Colombia had put in a special request for the Orrs to join them! Within a few months, Don and Vi were on a train headed for Richmond, Virginia, to be appointed as Southern Baptists' first music missionaries.

The first stop for almost any foreign missionary is language study. For the Orrs and others going to Latin America, this study was done in San José, Costa Rica. Don and Vi arrived there late in the summer of 1951 with their first child, Randy, who was only a few months old.

Spanish language study was for one year, but Don began using his music almost immediately. During that year, he directed the choir at the First Baptist Church in San José, a choir at the language school, and some music for radio programs. Vi sang a solo the first week she was there since she had studied two years of Spanish in high school.

Usually when language students finished their course in San José, they returned to the United States just long enough to get equipment or supplies; then they went straight to their appointed countries. Mr. and Mrs. Ben Welmaker did just that. They were in school with the Orrs, and they reached Colombia early in the fall of 1952. It seemed that the Orrs, however, had a bit of a problem.

For a whole year the Foreign Mission Board had tried, without success, to get the visas (government permits) the Orrs needed in order to enter and work in Colombia. From August through November, Don and Vi visited with their families, spoke in churches, prayed, and waited.

Early in December they received a letter from the Board.

"Still no visas—or much hope of getting them," Don read to his wife. "They want to know if we will consider going to a different country—maybe Brazil or Mexico."

"I don't feel we should do that, do you?" said Vi. "When God called us, we believed he had a special job for us to do in Colombia."

Don agreed. "It is hard to wait," he said, "but I will tell the Board to keep trying. If God wants us in Colombia, he will work it out."

Finally, in late January, they received permission to go.

"But the Board says there is still a problem," Don explained to his family. "We will have to go in first as tourists. That means no furniture or appliances—just what we can put in suitcases. Then we must travel to Ecuador and get regular visas there."

"Well, the Lord knows what he is doing. He has proved that to us many times," said Vi. "I think we can trust him to handle these details!"

# Beginning with the Basics

The plane trip to Colombia should have taken about one full day. It ended up taking more than three days.

First, the Orrs' plane was late leaving New Orleans, which caused them to miss their connection in Guatemala. They visited with missionaries there while waiting for the next day's flight.

From Guatemala, the Orrs flew on to Panama. On the way their son, Randy, came down with a high fever. Again they waited a day, until he was better.

Their next stop was Medellín [may-day-YEEN], Colombia. Their plane continued on to Cali [KAH-lee], the Orrs' final destination. It went without them, however, for a military official demanded their seats.

At last, on the fourth day, the pilot announced their final approach into Cali. Don and Vi strained at the window for a first glimpse of their new home. What they saw was a broad, beautiful, green river valley. The city is so close to the equator that plants are always very green. As the plane began to land, Don and Vi bowed their heads in prayer, thanking God for finally bringing them to this place where they were to serve him.

Don and Vi spent the first three or four days getting acquainted with Colombia and its people. The greenery they had seen from the air was nothing compared to what they found all around them on the ground. There were orchids, lilies, and ferns and vines of all

kinds. Poinsettias grew as big as trees! The Orrs also saw a plant with red heart-shaped flowers, anthurium. They saw orange, lemon, banana, and coffee trees. Many of them grew in people's yards!

The people of Colombia were colorful too. Many of them descended from the brown-skinned Indian tribes of Central and South America. Others, with lighter skin, were proud of their Spanish ancestors. Still others traced their roots to West Africa more than 300 years ago. In the city of Cali in 1953 were 250,000 of these people.

Southern Baptists had only been in Colombia about twelve years. The Roman Catholic Church was very strong there. Baptists and other "evangelicals" were not very welcome. In fact, some young people who accepted Christ as Savior and were baptized into Baptist or other evangelical churches were kicked out of their homes. Don and Vi Orr met some of these young believers during their first few days in the country.

Their friends, the Welmakers, made them feel welcome. But Don and Vi were eager to stop being tourists and really get settled. They made the trip to the border of Ecuador and back in two days. When they returned they had visas which would allow them to stay and work.

Their visas gave their occupation as "professor." One of their main jobs was to teach in a new seminary in Cali. The seminary would train church leaders for Colombia and nearby countries. But the seminary was not to open until the Orrs got there. And a school that had not opened could not officially hire two professors! For a while, to the government it looked like these two foreigners did not have jobs!

Someone suggested that the Baptist Day School, a primary school at one of the churches, had been operating for more than a year. The Orrs could be given contracts to teach there. This would satisfy the government. And so, for the first school term, Vi taught

English and Don taught musical notes and scales to children at the day school a few hours each week.

Just two weeks after they arrived in Cali, Don and Vi also started teaching in the new seminary. There were only three students at first and a total of five professors! But it was a beginning, and they would grow!

The Orrs' first home in Cali was an upstairs apartment, rented for them by the other missionaries. It had a little furniture in it, and Don and Vi bought the appliances and other things they had to have. The Foreign Mission Board helped with these expenses since they had not had to pay the usual cost of shipping everything from the United States.

When they had been in their new home about six months, Vi announced that they would have to move. "Today I caught Randy leaning over the rail of the balcony!" she told Don. "This place is just not safe for a two-year-old!"

They found a two-bedroom house all on the ground floor. It was owned by an officer in the Colombian air force. Like most Colombian houses, it had a tiny kitchen, a patio opening off the living room, and a wall all around the yard. When the officer found out that Don had been a pilot, he said, "Then *of course* I must rent the house to you!"

One of Vi's weekly chores was to shop for food in the market. The market was made up of a large number of shops and stalls crowded into a plaza. A plaza is an open space between buildings. People brought all kinds of foods there to sell. Buyers were expected to argue with the sellers until they could agree on a fair price.

None of these shops had refrigeration, and few of the sellers seemed to care about keeping their stalls clean. Raw meat hung from hooks in some stalls. Unwashed vegetables, straight from the fields, were piled in others. Damaged or rotten produce most often was simply thrown to the ground.

"You just can't imagine the dirt and the smell," Vi reported to Don after her first shopping trip. "It's enough to make you sick at your stomach."

"Unfortunately, we don't have much choice," Don reminded her. "There are no fancy supermarkets in Cali, and we can't afford to pay the high prices for the imported canned foods. Somehow you will have to get used to shopping in the market."

Week after week Vi went, and week after week she hated it. She prayed for God to give her strength and help her deal with this problem.

One day, as she was praying, God gave her the answer: "Don't look at all those vegetables. Don't look at the fruit or bloody meat or dirty floors. Look at the *people* selling those things. I gave myself for these people too. Look at the people, and love them as I do!"

With this new way of looking at things, Vi found she could look forward to market day. She saw it as a chance to make a new friend and share a witness for Jesus.

Some of the Colombian foods were quite different from anything the Orrs had had in Arkansas or Texas. After a while, several of these became family favorites. Almost every Thursday, for instance, they would have *sancocho* [sahn-KO-cho], a kind of stew made with chicken, plantains, yucca, and herbs. At noon on Saturdays they usually had *empanadas* [im-pah-NAH-dahs], which were similar to fried pies, but with a sort of hash inside. They also learned to eat a lot of rice, beans, and plantain, as the Colombians did. Plantain is a kind of banana, except larger and not as sweet. It is prepared in many ways, such as fried, baked, and in soups.

Vi found that their Colombian friends liked to try American foods. Some of their favorites were fried chicken, mashed potatoes, and apple pie.

Getting around the city of Cali was not easy in 1953. The roads were bumpy and unpaved. Cars cost a lot of money. Don had

**38**

ridden motorcycles when he was a teenager, so they bought one. Vi sometimes rode sidesaddle with him. She stopped riding when they learned she was expecting their second child. Ricky was born toward the end of that first year in Colombia.

Getting started in their music work proved to be one of the greatest challenges the Orrs faced. In the United States, most children were taught something about music as soon as they started school. Colombians at that time received almost no music education. The people loved to hear and sing music, but all they learned in school was the national anthem and a few folk songs. They could not tell one note from another of written music.

The Orrs discussed the problem. "We will really have to begin with the basics," said Vi.

"Yes, we cannot teach people to play piano or have chorus groups with harmony until they know about notes and scales," Don agreed. "We will have to start with 'do re mi' and work up from there."

"I believe the best way will be to start with children," said Vi. "We can start a children's choir at the First Baptist Church and continue to work with them. One day they will grow up to be good church musicians."

Don nodded. "That sounds good for the future, but it will take ten or fifteen years for those children to be old enough for the adult choir. Their parents need to learn to sing God's praises now. And we have students in the seminary who don't know any more about music than the boys and girls do. They must learn how to use music in worship so they can teach the churches where they serve after they graduate."

"We really have our work cut out for us," Vi said.

"We will just have to take each group where they are in their musical understanding and help them learn as much and as quickly as they can," Don added thoughtfully. "For the next few years, at least, we are going to have to try to do quite a few things at once!"

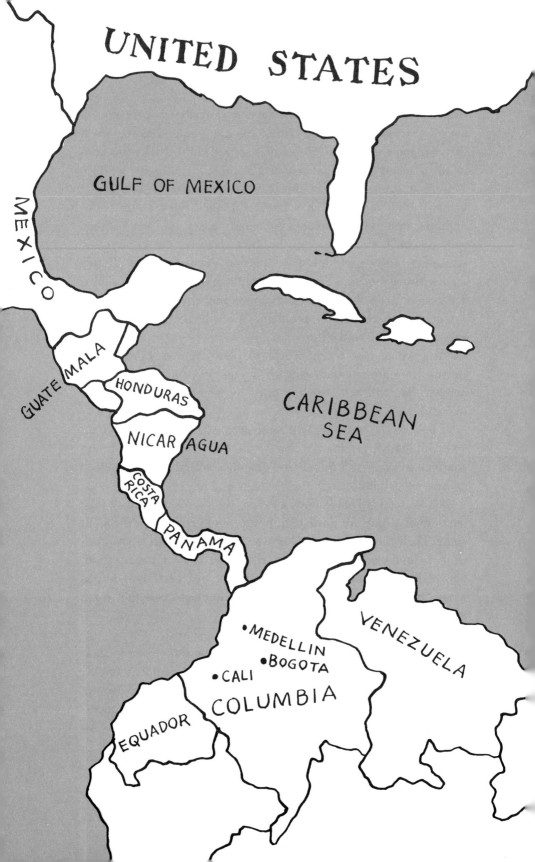

# Teaching Tomorrow's Church Leaders

"There is one thing you should understand about our people, Professor Orr." Don and one of his students were talking after a class at the seminary. "Most people here have never taken part in worship services. Most people attend the Catholic church. They are used to sitting and listening. Using congregational music in the Baptist church is new to them. But they like having a part in the services. It's a wonderful difference!"

Don and Vi had many things to learn as they started their work in Colombia. The difference between Catholic and Baptist church services was something they had not thought about in the United States. Now, however, they could see how this could be an important factor in their work.

They did not need anyone to tell them, though, about the importance of music in worship services. They remembered many services in which congregational hymns had helped prepare them for the sermons which followed. And they remembered hearing solos and choir specials that made them feel right in the presence of God! Most of their new Colombian friends, even those who had been Christians for some time, had never had such experiences. The Orrs hoped their teaching would help make such experiences possible for many Colombians.

The three students in the seminary that first year were joined by another three the next year. Then, as more people learned about

**41**

the school, the number of students began to grow rapidly. It was called the International Seminary because the missionaries hoped that pastors and church leaders would come from many countries in Central America and northern South America.

Classes met at first in the educational building of the First Baptist Church of Cali. The church was growing, though, just as the seminary was growing. Soon both of them needed more space.

The church had received a large donation from Maxey Jarman, an American businessman, for a new sanctuary. With Mr. Jarman's permission, they decided to use the money for an educational building. They also agreed to share part of the building with the seminary.

Ben Welmaker was chosen as the seminary's first president. He was very pleased about the space they would have in the new building, which had four floors. On the ground floor was the day school. The church used all of the second floor, while the seminary used the third. The fourth floor was mostly open space, which could be a gymnasium one day or an auditorium for a large meeting the next day. At times both the church and the seminary were able to put that extra space to good use.

Don and Vi felt they were just getting started in their work at the seminary when the time came for their first furlough. That year in the United States gave them a chance for some good visits with their families, especially for the grandparents to get to know Randy and Ricky. It also gave the Orrs an opportunity to share with many churches the ways God had led them and the exciting progress being made at the seminary. Thinking about that, though, made them anxious to get back to Colombia.

Not long after the Orrs' return, the seminary reached a record enrollment of seventy-five students. The young men and women came from Colombia and fourteen other countries. Venezuela and Ecuador, Colombia's neighbors to the east and south, both were well represented at the school.

**43**

Almost every student had to start his music education with Don's course on music theory and sight reading. Don also introduced students to conducting, planning worship services, and understanding what a music ministry could mean to a church. Sometimes he taught courses in religious education, especially how to have a good Sunday School and Training Union.

Vi's teaching usually included instruction in piano, voice, drama, and how to work with children's choirs. She also gave singing and piano lessons to individual students.

In addition to classes, Don organized a choir among the seminary students. Vi helped by translating many hymns and choruses into Spanish. Both of them often sang solos and duets for chapel, church, and community programs.

With so many students, the seminary needed a permanent home. Don was asked to be in charge of the construction since he had supervised construction of a second church in Cali. For most of the next year, he worked on building an administration building, three dormitories, and a utility building that housed a carpenter shop.

As part of the construction, Don took on one more project.

"I think it is time the Orrs had a permanent home too," he told Vi. "We can put it on that property right in front of the seminary."

"Can we design it just the way we want it?" Vi asked.

"Yes, so long as we include those things the Mission says we should have," Don replied.

"You mean like a living room large enough for meetings? I would want that anyway. To have different groups come into our home will just make it that much more special!" said Vi. "I would love to be able to have all the missionaries over for our annual Christmas party. And we could have our neighbors in for home concerts! We have lived in six different houses since we arrived in Colombia, but none of them had that much room!"

Native stone was used to cover the outside of the house. It was a

**45**

one-story house with all the room Vi wanted. A special feature was a chimney built of white stone.

Just about the time the house was finished, a fifth member joined the Orr family. In 1958 Roger became the third boy in the house. By this time Ricky and Randy attended an English-language international school in Cali. Their classmates included boys and girls from all over the world.

The seminary had just begun using its new buildings when President Welmaker called a meeting of all the teachers.

"I have been over the enrollments for next term," he told them, "and it looks like we will do well to have fifty students this time. The big difference is in the number of students from other countries."

"What's happened?" everyone wanted to know. "Don't they think we are doing a good job of training their young people?"

"That isn't the problem," Ben assured them. "What has happened is that Baptists in several of these countries are setting up their own training programs."

"But why?" someone aked. "The Foreign Mission Board has always said it was better to have one strong seminary than a half dozen weak ones."

"I still think that is a good idea, but we need to see the problems these other countries have," the president continued. "You all know that some foreign students have had trouble getting government permission to come here to study. And most of you know several such students who have studied with us and then gone to work in a church here in Colombia. Baptists in Venezuela and the other countries now feel that the best way to prepare their young people to serve in their own churches is to give them training close to home."

"Well, we still have plenty of work to do training leaders for our churches in Colombia," Don observed.

Ben nodded. "Yes, in fact some of the other denominations with churches here have asked about sending some of their pastors to our school. And one of these days those students from other countries may decide they need to come here for advanced training. In the meantime, we will all need to work at giving the best education we can to these fifty students. We want them well prepared to serve the churches."

# A Laboratory in a Church

From the time they arrived in Colombia, Don and Vi knew they had a big job to do. They believed that their work as music missionaries involved more than just teaching in the seminary.

"We must help all the churches. They need to learn to use more music," said Vi. "Most of them are using little hymnbooks with only the words in them. The music part has to come from memory!"

"They really cannot use printed music right now. First they have to know what the notes stand for," Don pointed out. "It will be our job to teach them, with the help of the other missionaries."

The Orrs were the only missionaries assigned to work in music full time. But many of the missionary wives did what they could where they worked. Some of them gave piano lessons or led small church choirs or started children's choirs.

Then, the Orrs decided to travel around the country, working in churches. They spent a week at a time working with just one church. They would meet with the whole congregation and then with smaller groups of persons. The people learned about notes and how they worked together to create music. These weeks reminded Don a little of his days as a summer field-worker, but there was so much to try to teach these people in such a short time.

Sometimes Vi got discouraged. "I wonder if we are really doing any good at all with a week like this. It seems they just begin to get the idea when we have to leave them. They hear us sing and get a taste for what music in the church can be like. Then we leave!"

"Giving them that taste is important though," Don noted. "It helps them want to learn more and improve their church's music. But I agree that there must be some other way."

Don and Vi found another way almost on their own doorstep.

They had always taken an active part in the First Baptist Church of Cali. Don served as minister of music and Sunday School director. Vi taught a Sunday School class. They both worked from time to time in some of the missions sponsored by the church.

The Orrs were already *doing* the new idea before they ever put it into words.

"We've been trying to teach the churches about a good music program," said Don. "Why not just *show* them?"

"And use our own church as the model!" exclaimed Vi. "Of course, First is larger than most churches, but at least the others could see some of the things that are possible!"

"There's something else too," Don added. "We can use the church as a sort of laboratory, trying out new music or new approaches here before sharing them with our seminary students or the people in other churches."

Two "demonstration groups" already were going well. Don had worked with the adult choir for a long time. They still were not great musicians, but they had made a lot of progress. Often Don used them to introduce new hymns to the congregation. The choir would sing the new hymn as "special music" during a Sunday morning service. Then, perhaps a month later, Don would use it as a congregational hymn.

Vi worked every week with children in the children's choir. She did what she had said needed to be done, starting with children and helping them grow to become fine church musicians. Again she found that she had to translate music for the boys and girls to sing since not much was available in Spanish.

Many of the children were very faithful in their attendance—

including, of course, the Orrs' sons. During the family's second furlough in the United States, their fourth child, Roxanna, was born. Vi was happy to have a girl and another soprano in the family at last! Roxanna later developed a lovely solo voice.

When both Roger and Roxanna were teenagers, the Orrs started a youth choir at First Baptist Church. This became one of the most active areas of their work in the church. Don and Vi searched for the best musical pieces being written. They used music from the United States and Latin America. They looked for words and music they thought the young people would enjoy. Sometimes Don, as the director, had to get used to a different kind of beat.

The youth choir sang regularly in the church services. At least once a year, they prepared and presented a musical drama or other special program.

"This is a wonderful group of young people. Many of them are 'second-generation' musicians," Vi observed one night after choir practice. "At least half of them have come up through my children's choir. And there is quite a number of them whose *parents* were in my first children's choir."

"I can really tell the difference too," said Don. "I believe their tone is better than choirs in the past, and it is much easier to introduce new music with them."

The spirit among the young people in the choir was at least partly a reflection of their leaders. Don reminded them that every time they sang they were telling someone about the good news of Jesus.

Introducing handbells to Baptists in Colombia had both its good and bad side for Don. Certainly the bells had a beautiful tone. It was also true that the bells created interest and excitement wherever they were played. On the other hand, those bells were heavy, especially when boxed up together. And Don most often got the job of hauling them from place to place. Soon he had a handbell group among the young people at the church and the

**52**

students at the seminary. Many times they played before churches or other groups who were hearing handbells for the very first time.

Don and Vi's music participation at the church did not end with the choirs. During almost any week, they sang solos before some group. They also were involved frequently—as either singers or directors—with various duets, trios, quartets, sextets, and octets, or ensembles! It seemed that every way they turned they found another opportunity to use music for God, either to praise him or to tell others about him.

# A Few Milestones

"Here's a ticket stub from the Municipal Theatre back in 1964. Do you remember what that was about?" asked Vi. She was digging through their family scrapbook.

"That would have to be one of the first times we did the *Messiah* for the community. You sang *two* different solo parts!" Don recalled.

"We had at least sixty people in the chorus that night. They represented close to a dozen countries."

"When you think about it, it's surprising that the audience got anything out of it since we did it all in English," said Don.

"They all seemed to enjoy it though, and we got good write-ups in the newspaper!"

"There was a good reason behind those write-ups. We gave all the ticket money to the campaign to start a Cali symphony," Don reminded her. "That was the first time the newspaper really mentioned our seminary. I suppose they would not have mentioned it, even then, if you and I had not sung the solos!"

"But they did mention us," Vi pointed out. "The fact that we could have the program at all was important. It showed that the persecution of evangelicals was pretty well over by that time."

"Say, here's something that fell out of the scrapbook. It's a copy of that citation given to us by the Southern Baptist Church Music Conference."

"That was in 1978," said Vi. "Our seminary graduating class observed its twenty-fifth anniversary the same year. You directed a special music program as part of the celebration!"

"Going to Atlanta to receive that citation during the annual meeting of the music conference was a great honor! They gave us lifetime memberships in the organization because we were the first music missionaries. Really, though, I felt that we were representing all music missionaries. Now close to one hundred music missionaries serve in forty countries around the world!"

"Yes, it's wonderful to think about all that has happened over these years," Vi agreed. "I particularly like this line on the citation: 'In gratitude to our Lord for that which has been accomplished in his name and for his glory.' We have known that God brought us to Colombia for a special purpose, or we might have given up and gone home!"

"Here is a photograph of me on crutches in 1965. That should remind us that it hasn't always been easy," said Don. "My knee was really messed up. I thought I was going to be stiff legged for the rest of my life!"

"But then the prayers of so many friends helped us. And God brought healing to your leg," Vi recalled. "I will always count that as one of God's miracles!"

"What about the time I broke both arms in that motorcycle accident? And that was just after I had had surgery on my back!" Don laughed. "God has managed to keep me on the job, but he has really had to work at it!"

"Look at the pictures on these two pages," said Vi. "They are from that pageant we did in 1980 to help introduce the new hymnal."

"I remember. Our nice 500-page Spanish *Baptist Hymnal* had just been published. Getting our people to start using it was a real step forward!"

**56**

"Here's a picture of the giant-sized model of the hymnal. Hector Ramirez made it for us," Vi pointed out.

"He really worked hard to get every detail right," said Don. "When that hymnal stepped out on stage during your pageant, it looked just like the real thing. Who is this supposed to be in this picture?"

"That's our version of Ira Sankey. He was one of several hymn composers and writers featured in our pageant. See that big top hat and cane? And here's John Newton dressed as a ship's captain. And blind Fannie Crosby. And cowboy singer Stuart Hamblin. They all are represented among the hymns in the book."

"And this boy over here?"

"That is Claudio Cardenas. I had him representing the youth of today. God has given them many talents. One day they may contribute hymns they have written to some future hymnal."

"You know," said Don, "God has blessed our ministry here. I can think of many people whose lives have been touched through music."

"Yes, there are so many," Vi agreed. "Remember Fanny dePerez? She was just a young teenager the day she stepped inside a church to listen to a choir practicing for a special program. When she came back on the day of the program, she heard the good news of Jesus and accepted him as her Savior. Later she took piano lessons, enrolled in the seminary, and married one of the students. Now she is our national WMU president and her husband is executive secretary of our convention!"

"Or how about Hugo Parra?" asked Don. "He attended your children's choir when his father first brought him to church. Now he is a deacon, church treasurer, and sings bass in my adult choir!"

"And don't forget Rafaela Monzano," added Vi. "She was a student in the Baptist Day School when we first came to Cali. Then

**57**

she was in my first children's choir. Now she and her husband both sing in the adult choir, and all five of her children are active in our choir program too!"

"I suppose only God can count all the times when music has opened the door for people to come to know him," said Don. "We really could not ask for more than to be used by him!"

# A New Day; a New Way

Don and Vi have been in Colombia for more than twenty-five years. They still find new ways to serve.

The Orrs are members of the First Baptist Church of Cali where Ramon Medina [rah-MOHN meh-DEE-nah] is pastor. He encourages different groups to be in charge of the worship service at times.

One day a group of the men met to make plans for the Sunday when they would be in charge. Three of the men agreed to preach brief sermons. Then Don suggested, "How would you like to have a choir of all men on that Sunday?"

All those at the meeting liked the idea, even though they had not seen that done. The men met twice for practice. About twenty-six men participated in the men's choir that Sunday, singing special numbers in both the morning and evening services.

The church members liked the men's choir very much. They had never heard a large group of men sing together like that. They asked when the men could sing again.

Don knew that few of the men could read music. This helped give him another idea.

"Pastor, since Training Union is supposed to be training for church membership," he said, "why can't we have one group set up for learning about music? They could learn to read music. Then

**59**

when these people sing in a choir, they will be able to learn each piece more easily."

So the class was begun. Soon it included members from the adult, youth, and men's choirs. Don taught them about notes and explained which line each voice part should sing.

Other new doors opened for the Orrs' music ministry in connection with Easter during 1981 and 1982.

One new opportunity began with a young man in First Baptist who is a part-time radio announcer. He spoke to a Catholic priest about using the youth choir on his 72-hour radio marathon show Easter weekend. The priest, Father Hurtado [oor-TAH-doh], was interested enough to schedule them for about ten minutes on Friday.

When Don and the youth choir arrived at the studio, Father Hurtado was busy playing records over the air. The young people got ready to sing and then, as usual, had a time of prayer together.

As the youth choir sang the numbers they had prepared, the priest was impressed with their musical skill. He was even more impressed with their youth and enthusiasm.

Father Hurtado told his radio audience, "I know you can hear these young people, but I wish you could be here in the studio with me. I wish you could have seen them before they came in to sing. These young people are different. We adults are wrong when we think that all young people are interested only in drugs and things of this world.

"I wish you could have joined me to hear them pray before they came in here to sing for you on the radio. In fact, I would like for some of them to pray right now."

And so, live on the radio, several of them did!

During the next break, the priest asked the group to stay and sing some more later. Don and the young people began to tell him about their handbells.

**60**

"I have never heard of these," said the priest, "but could you bring them to the studio?"

There were thirty-nine bells in the set, with twelve young people to ring them. Don was not at all sure they could fit into the small studio, but somehow they managed.

Father Hurtado asked for more on Saturday and ended up using them for five hours of broadcast time! During part of that time, he invited Pastor Medina to speak to the radio audience.

On Easter Sunday the youth choir was to sing a cantata during the morning worship service at First Baptist Church. They invited the priest to come hear them. And he did! He walked right to the front of the church, tape recorder in hand. Pastor Medina invited him to come up to the pulpit and speak to the congregation.

Many of the church members did not know what to think. They had never seen a Catholic priest in a Baptist church before. Some of them remembered problems between Catholics and evangelicals in the past.

Father Hurtado congratulated the church on its program and its young people. He told them they should be very proud of their youth choir. Then he sat down front and recorded the whole service.

At the close of the service, an announcement was made that the adult choir would sing another cantata in the evening service. The priest asked Don, "May I come back for that one too?"

"Certainly, if you wish," Don told him.

When time for the service came, Father Hurtado and his tape recorder were right down front again.

Because of the 1981 radio program, another member of the church was able to get a friend to consider using the youth choir on a television show. No Baptist group such as this had ever been on television in Colombia.

The people from the television show decided to tape three numbers each by the choir and the handbell group. They recorded the sound in the studio. Then they took the group up on a nearby mountain for some outdoor shots.

The program was shown during prime time on the Friday before Easter, 1982, on a variety show called "The Great Show of Isadora." Isadora, a popular singer in Colombia, introduced the choir herself. She said, "I have been particularly impressed by the dedication and sincerity of these young people. They really mean what they are singing!"

Through the work of Don and Vi Orr and many others, music missions continues to open doors to the sharing of the good news of Jesus in Colombia and around the world.

# Remember

God began to prepare Don and Vi Orr for service as music missionaries long before they had any idea of what he wanted them to do. What were some of the talents and experiences he gave them which made them better missionaries?

The Orrs faced several problems during their lives. What did they say was the one thing which kept them from turning back from their missionary service?

The Orrs have said, "We are missionaries first and then musicians." Why do you think that is important?

What are some special talents and experiences you can think of that God has given you?

How can you use these to share the good news of Jesus with people you know?

# About the Author

Lee Hollaway grew up as the son of Southern Baptist missionaries in Japan. He claims Arkansas as his home state and attended Ouachita College and Southwestern Seminary, as Mr. Orr did. He now lives in Tennessee, where he is the director of communications for the Seminary External Education Division of the six Southern Baptist seminaries. Between 1970 and 1977 he was editor of *Crusader*, the magazine for Royal Ambassadors in grades one through six. He has written four other books for children. You may be able to find some of them in your church library.